# URANIUM

# North American Natural Resources

Coal

Copper

Freshwater Resources

Gold and Silver

Iron

Marine Resources

Natural Gas

Oil

Renewable Energy

Salt

Timber and Forest Products

Uranium

## NORTH AMERICAN NATURAL RESOURCES

# URANIUM

## John Perritano

MASON CREST

Mason Crest
450 Parkway Drive, Suite D
Broomall, PA 19008
www.masoncrest.com

MTM Publishing, Inc.
435 West 23rd Street, #8C
New York, NY 10011
www.mtmpublishing.com

President: Valerie Tomaselli
Vice President, Book Development: Hilary Poole
Designer: Annemarie Redmond
Illustrator: Richard Garratt
Copyeditor: Peter Jaskowiak
Editorial Assistant: Andrea St. Aubin

Series ISBN: 978-1-4222-3378-8
ISBN: 978-1-4222-3390-0
Ebook ISBN: 978-1-4222-8564-0

Library of Congress Cataloging-in-Publication Data
Perritano, John.
  Uranium / by John Perritano.
    pages cm.— (North American natural resources)
  ISBN 978-1-4222-3390-0 (hardback)—ISBN 978-1-4222-3378-8 (series)—ISBN
978-1-4222-8564-0 (ebook)
1.  Uranium—North America—Juvenile literature.  I. Title.
  TN490.U7P456 2015
  333.8'549320973—dc23
                        2015005856

Printed and bound in the United States of America.

First printing
9 8 7 6 5 4 3 2 1

# TABLE OF CONTENTS

## Key Icons to Look for:

**Words to Understand:** These words with their easy-to-understand definitions will increase the reader's understanding of the text, while building vocabulary skills.

**Sidebars:** This boxed material within the main text allows readers to build knowledge, gain insights, explore possibilities, and broaden their perspectives by weaving together additional information to provide realistic and holistic perspectives.

**Research Projects:** Readers are pointed toward areas of further inquiry connected to each chapter. Suggestions are provided for projects that encourage deeper research and analysis.

**Text-Dependent Questions:** These questions send the reader back to the text for more careful attention to the evidence presented there.

**Series Glossary of Key Terms:** This back-of-the-book glossary contains terminology used throughout the series. Words found here increase the reader's ability to read and comprehend higher-level books and articles in this field.

*Note to Educator: As publishers, we feel it's our role to give young adults the tools they need to thrive in a global society. To encourage a more worldly perspective, this book contains both imperial and metric measurements as well as references to a wider global context. We hope to expose the readers to the most common conversions they will come across outside of North America.*

## Major Uranium Deposits in North America

Uranium Deposit
Site Mentioned in Text

*Davis Strait*

*Hudson Bay*

C
A
N
A
D
A

McArthur River Mine

Chalk River
Laboratories

Arco, Idaho

Three Mile Island
Nuclear Generating
Station

Yucca Mountain

U N I T E D   S T A T E S
O F   A M E R I C A

University of Chicago

Navajo Nation

Pittsylvania County, Virginia

Los Alamos
National
Laboratory

PACIFIC
OCEAN

ATLANTIC
OCEAN

*Gulf of Mexico*

M E X I C O

0 km   500   1,000
0 miles      500

*Caribbean Sea*

0 km   500   1,000   1,500
0 miles      500      1,000

# INTRODUCTION

Uranium has many faces, and it packs quite a punch. It is a source of immense energy and wonder. It is shiny and bright, just like silver, but if you were to pick a chunk of it up, you'd find it very weighty—19 times as heavy as an equal volume of water.

In fact, uranium is the heaviest element in nature—and the most energetic. When uranium atoms are split through a process called fission, they can light a town, power a submarine, or destroy a city.

**An abandoned uranium mine in Utah. (XScream1/Dreamstime)**

Uranium is also precious because it is not always easy to find: almost all the world's uranium comes from only a handful of countries, including Kazakhstan (the largest producer), Canada, Australia, Russia, Niger, Namibia, and the United States.

Don't get too close, though. Uranium sheds particles known as radiation that could kill you. Yet when doctors use special machines to control the release of these high-energy particles, they can cure people of diseases and provide a more accurate diagnosis on what ails a patient.

Uranium has reshaped modern history, influenced the thoughts and actions of political leaders, and inspired science-fiction novelists and filmmakers. In uranium, unlike any other element, we see the best and worst humankind has to offer. The element has the capacity to move science to new frontiers, while also fueling the ultimate weapon of terror.

## Chapter One

# HISTORY

"*Daren habe ich gar nicht gedacht!*" Albert Einstein exclaimed in his native German. Translated into English, this means, "I never thought of that!"

It was a startling admission by Einstein, one of history's greatest scientists and thinkers. Einstein sat in his summer cottage on Long Island, responding to the fantastic tale spun by two of his friends, the Hungarian physicists Leo Szilard and Eugene Wigner. The men were visiting Einstein on a matter of grave urgency: to discuss the technical aspects of splitting atoms.

## Words to Understand

**compound:** two or more elements chemically bound together.

**fission:** splitting the nucleus of an atom, which then releases energy.

**isotope:** each of two or more forms of a chemical element with the same atomic number but different numbers of neutrons.

**neutron:** an elementary particle without an electrical charge.

**radiation:** energy emitted in the form of particles by radioactive substances.

**theoretically:** dealing with a theory, or based on a theory.

It was July 1939, several months after the German physicist Otto Frisch proved that uranium atoms could split when struck by a **neutron**. Frisch called the process **fission**. In retelling Frisch's theory, the *New York Times* described uranium as a "cannonball" that could yield "the greatest amount of atomic energy so far liberated by man on earth." In other words, it was now **theoretically** possible to unleash the thunderous force bound up in that atom, producing the most deadly weapon in human history—the atomic bomb.

Einstein's Hungarian visitors described in great detail how a slow-moving neutron aimed at the center of uranium isotope 235 (U-235) could trigger a reaction that

## A Vision of Catastrophe

"The unleashed power of the atom has changed everything save our modes of thinking, and we thus drift toward unparalleled catastrophes."

—Albert Einstein, August 2, 1964

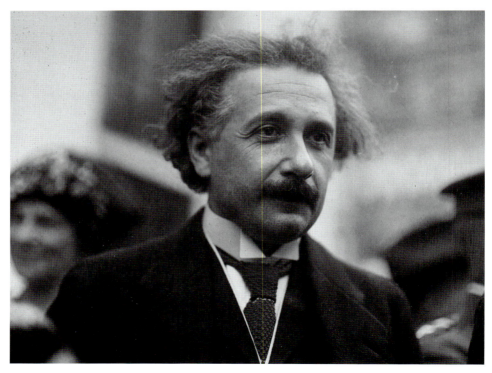

**Albert Einstein.**

would unleash millions upon millions of volts of electricity and begin an uncontrolled nuclear reaction. Before such a weapon could be built, however, scientists had to overcome many technical problems.

Einstein listened as his visitors discussed what would happen if the Nazis developed the atom bomb first. Einstein nodded, understanding the implications. He agreed to sign a letter to Franklin Roosevelt, the president of the United States, urging him to take action. In the letter, Einstein and his colleagues warned Roosevelt that Germany could build "a single bomb," which if "carried by boat and exploded in port, might very well destroy the whole port together with some of the surrounding territory."

The race to harness the explosive power of uranium was on. Einstein would later regret signing the letter because of the awesome consequences the atomic bomb would have on the world. He reportedly called the letter "the greatest mistake" of his life.

## New Planet, New Element

Humans did not begin their relationship with uranium in Long Island or Germany for that matter, but in the Middle Ages, an era of history that lasted from the 5th century to the 15th century. Miners in Bohemia, in what is today the Czech Republic, were searching for silver. As they chopped at the walls of earthen mine shafts with their picks and chisels, the miners noticed a dark, greasy, tar-like material sticking to the pointed ends of their tools.

The miners called the substance *pechblende*, a combination of two German words, *pech*, which means "tar" or "misfortune," and *blende*, which means "mineral." The English called the black substance "pitchblende." Whatever its name, the miners discarded the kidney-shaped globs as worthless. Silver, after all, was the real treasure.

Eventually, the mines of Bohemia ran dry, but the pitchblende remained. Over the years, many people grew sick with a mysterious disease that caused them to cough up blood. Their bodies wasted away as "their lungs rot," said the German scientist Georgius Agricola. He blamed this "mountain disease" on "pestilential air" in the mine shafts.

Pitchblende (the black bands) in uranium ore.

No one at the time linked the ailments to the black tar that the miners pulled out of the earth. However, one of those rocks eventually found its way into the hands of Martin Klaproth, a would-be Catholic priest who had taught himself chemistry. In 1789, Klaproth examined the pitchblende and purified it into a "new element which I see as a strange kind of half-metal." Klaproth's new element created vibrant shades of greens and yellows when he added it to glass.

Klaproth could have named the element after himself, but he didn't. Instead, he named it *uranium*, after the newly discovered planet, Uranus, which was named for the Greek god of the sky. Klaproth, however, had not discovered uranium in its pure form—what he found was a **compound** of the element that's present in pitchblende, a black mineral consisting mainly of uranium oxide. It wasn't until in 1841 that a French chemist, Eugène Péligot, isolated pure uranium.

## Invisible Rays

No one paid much attention to the mysterious element until 1896, when Antoine-Henri Becquerel discovered that uranium gave off powerful, invisible rays. Becquerel came from a family of distinguished scholars and scientists. His father, Alexandre-Edmond Becquerel, had researched solar **radiation** and phosphorescence, which is the emission of light without heat.

**Uranium glass from the mid-19th century, in the Teylers Museum, the Netherlands.**

## Marie Curie

In 1903, Marie Curie became the first woman to win the Nobel Prize in physics. She, alongside her husband and Henri Becquerel, was awarded for accomplishments in the study of radioactivity. She won a second Nobel in 1911 in chemistry. Curie died in 1934 after years of working with radioactive elements. She died of aplastic anemia, a blood disease in which the body stops making new blood cells. The malady is often caused by prolonged exposure to radiation.

**Marie Curie.**

At the time, the younger Becquerel wanted to known whether there was any connection between newly discovered X-rays and phosphorescence. A year before, the German physicist Wilhelm Conrad Röntgen accidently discovered X-rays, which he then used to photograph the bones in his wife's hand.

Fascinated with the discovery, Becquerel placed uranium salts near a photographic plate covered with dark paper. After a while, a "fogged" image appeared on the plate. Henri Becquerel understood immediately that uranium was giving off some unseen force. His discovery caught the interests of Marie Curie and her husband, Pierre. While working in their Paris laboratory, the Curies worked hard to find out which elements in pitchblende gave off the extraordinary rays.

While studying the rays, the Curies made a number of important discoveries. They learned that some elements in pitchblende emitted invisible rays that they called radiation. Radiation is the natural process by which atoms spontaneously disintegrate into energy.

The Curies discovered that two elements in pitchblende, *polonium*, named after Marie's home country of Poland, and *radium*, were giving off radioactive rays. The Curies and Becquerel also showed that uranium was radioactive. It had positive, negative, and neutral electrical charges. The rays given off by the elements could travel through paper, wood, and even metal.

By 1930, scientists understood that uranium could be a source of immense energy, if only they could figure out how to release it. In 1938, Otto Hahn and Fritz Strassmann, scientists working in Nazi Germany, successfully split the uranium atom. This ultimately caught the attention of Einstein and the two visitors to his summer cottage. Soon after, Franklin Roosevelt took Einstein's advice and ordered scientists in the United States to begin their own experiments on uranium, which in 1942 resulted in the first controlled nuclear reaction.

Three years later, using a highly enriched **isotope** of uranium, U-235, the United States exploded the first atomic bomb during a test in the blistering hot New Mexican desert. At the time, World War II was ending. The United States and its allies, Great Britain and the Soviet Union, had vanquished both Italy and Nazi Germany. Although the war in Europe was over, the fight against the third Axis power, Japan, was still raging in the Pacific.

On August 6, 1945, an American plane called the *Enola Gay* dropped the first atomic bomb on the Japanese city of Hiroshima, killing tens of thousands. The bomb was nicknamed "Little Boy." Three days later, the Americans dropped another atom bomb, "Fat Man," on another Japanese city, Nagasaki. The Japanese, seeing the awesome power of the unleashed atom, surrendered on August 15.

## Splitting Atoms

Atoms split during a process known as fission. Fission occurs when a neutron from one atom hits the nucleus of another atom. When that happens, atoms release more neutrons that strike more atoms, creating a chain reaction. As the atoms split, they spit out a huge amount of energy. That's because when uranium atoms split, they lose mass. According to Einstein, the more mass an atom has, the more energy it can create. Uranium has a lot of mass because of the number of protons and neutrons in its atom. This means each atom has a lot of matter to lose, and therefore a lot of energy to expel.

The bombing of Nagasaki, on August 9, 1945, as seen from the air.

These events would shape the world we live in today. Other countries, notably the Soviet Union, developed their own nuclear weapons for their own armies. Several times the world's nuclear powers came to the brink of atomic war, which could have resulted in global destruction on an immense scale. As the specter of nuclear war hung over the planet, scientists soon began figuring out how to use uranium for peaceful purposes.

## TEXT-DEPENDENT QUESTIONS

1. How does fission work?
2. Which scientist first discovered uranium?
3. What is phosphorescence?
4. What gives uranium its mass?

## RESEARCH PROJECTS

1. The energy emitted by uranium is a form of electromagnetic radiation. Research and write an essay describing the different types of electromagnetic radiation. Describe what each form of electromagnetic radiation does. What are their similarities? What are their differences?
2. Pick one of the scientists mentioned in the text and create a timeline of his or her life.

## Chapter Two

# EXTRACTION

### Words to Understand

**fusion:** the process by which atoms combine, creating an enormous amount of energy.

**Geiger counter:** an instrument used to measure the intensity of radiation by detecting particles from radioactive substances.

**in situ:** in something's original place.

**leach:** to drain a substance away from soil by dissolving it in a liquid.

**magma:** molten rock deep within Earth.

**tailings:** waste products left over after ore has been extracted from rock.

**ore:** naturally occurring mineral from which metal can be extracted.

Uranium, like other elements, is very difficult to extract from the Earth. That's because it is never found free in nature, but bound up in more than 100 different **ores**. While these ores are widely distributed across the planet, very few deposits are rich in uranium. About 20 countries are home to uranium mines, although just 6 countries—Kazakhstan, Canada, Australia, Niger, Namibia, and Russia—produce most of the world's mined uranium.

Uranium came to Earth as an alien from outer space, when one or more massive stars exploded, showering the planet with different elements. Those exploding stars are called supernova. Stars, including our Sun, are big balls of super-heated gas. They get this enormous energy through **fusion,** a nuclear reaction that joins the nuclei of atoms. Fusion takes place deep inside stars as they convert hydrogen to helium. The process releases so much energy that the stars shine and give off an immense amount of heat.

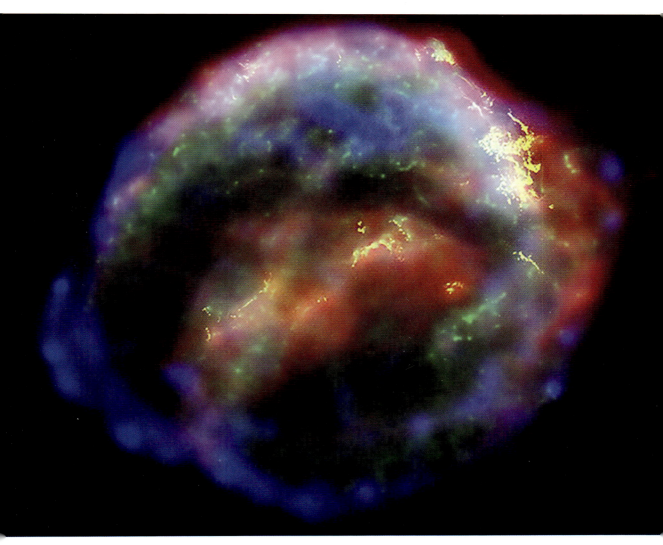

**The remnants (or leftovers) of Kepler's Supernova, named for the astronomer Johannes Kepler, who observed the supernova in 1604.**

A star begins to die when it uses up all its hydrogen and helium fuel. When that happens, the star starts to convert most of its atoms to iron. When fusion stops, gravity forces the star to collapse on itself, releasing a huge amount of energy. Eventually, as the star erupts in a supernova, it sends out billions of atoms of various elements into space.

Some of those atoms showered down on Earth as the planet formed. In fact, most of our planet's carbon, oxygen, nitrogen, silicon, and iron came from supernova

Uranium ore.

explosions. Because those explosions were so hot, newer and heavier elements, including uranium and gold, formed within the blast. Those elements also rained down on Earth, seeding the planet.

## Finding Uranium

Although uranium is an unusually heavy metal, it never sank deep into Earth's core, as some other elements did. Instead, uranium concentrated itself in very small amounts on Earth's crust. Many uranium deposits can be found in sedimentary rock, such as shale. Sedimentary rock forms in layers over time at the bottom of oceans and lakes. As time passes, the weight of the upper layers squeezes the bottom layers, forming solid rock.

Uranium is also found in granite, the igneous rock that makes up Earth's continents. Igneous rock forms when volcanic eruptions force **magma** to the surface. The hot liquids containing uranium push through cracks in the rocks, eventually cooling and solidifying into minerals with a high metal content.

## Mining for Ore

Mining for uranium is no different than mining for other elements, including gold, copper, and silver. In fact, finding uranium ore is easier than finding ore containing these other elements. That's partly because uranium is more abundant than silver and gold. Moreover, uranium also decays over time and emits radiation. It is easy to spot radiation using special machines such as **Geiger counters**. They also use a device known as a scintillometer to find uranium deposits from greater distances. The scintillometer detects gamma rays, high-energy electromagnetic radiation, that uranium gives off.

### McArthur River Mine

The world's largest uranium mine is the McArthur River Mine, located in Saskatchewan, Canada. Uranium was first discovered there in 1988. Fourteen years later, the mine became the world's largest producer of mined uranium.

**A Geiger counter is used to measure radiation. Sometimes this is done to find uranium to mine; other times it's done for safety reasons—to check places, people, or even food that might have been exposed to radiation.**

When miners find the ore, they dig it out of the ground in one of two ways: through open-pit mining when the uranium is close to the surface, or by digging underground mines when it is not. Miners carve out open-pit mines in vertical sections of rock called *benches*, which look like a series of steps. Most of the uranium mines in Canada are open-pits. Miners dig underground mines when ore is deep in the ground. Underground mines are not as intrusive or as environmentally damaging as open-pit mines. Whichever way it is extracted, mineralogists can tell whether ore has a lot of uranium by measuring its radioactivity.

## Special Techniques

Miners often use special techniques to extract uranium. One of these techniques is called **in situ** leach mining, or solution mining. Most uranium mines in the United States use this method. Here's how it works: Instead of extracting uranium ore from the ground, miners leave the ore soaking in groundwater, where the minerals dissolve. Engineers then inject various solutions, including hydrogen peroxide and sulfuric acid, into the groundwater through a series of wells. They then pump the ore-rich solution to the surface. Once the solution is recovered, miners can easily extract the uranium.

Heap leaching is a technique miners use when there's not a lot of uranium in ore. During the process, the mined ore is pulverized into small chunks and stacked into mounds nearly 100 feet (30.4 meters) high. Those mountains of ore sit on top of a waterproof plastic or clay liner. Engineers drip acid on to the pile over a series of

**Uranium mine and processing plant, northern Canada.**

weeks, or sometimes months. The solution flows through the pile, causing uranium and other elements to **leach** out. This creates a soup of dissolved uranium, which can then be recovered. Engineers can then recycle the remaining solution and pour it again on another pile.

## Arms Race

Global demand for uranium grew in the 1950s when the United States and Soviet Union were locked in a bitter arms race that came to symbolize the Cold War, an ideological battle between communism and the Western democracies. Eventually, the cost of maintaining and building nuclear weapons, coupled with domestic economic problems, contributed to the breakup of the Soviet Union into many other countries.

From the 1950s to the 1980s, many people feared a possible nuclear war between the United States and the Soviet Union. Many people invested in supplies and fallout shelters, in hopes of surviving.

**Highly enriched uranium, from the Y-12 National Security Complex in Oak Ridge, Tennessee.**

## Yellowcake

Extracting uranium from its many ores is a complicated process. When workers remove ore from the ground, they truck it to a mill, where huge machines beat the rock into a powder. This process, called milling, results in only few pounds of uranium from each ton of ore.

The ore is crushed into fine sand and treated with chemicals, including sulfuric acid, to remove impurities. Since uranium ores vary from place to place, different chemicals have to be used in different places. As the milling process continues, the **tailings** taken away in trucks ands stored.

After milling, mining companies sell pure uranium to others who will enrich the element. During the enrichment process, uranium is refined until it turns into a bright-colored, clay-like material called *yellowcake*. Yellowcake contains 70 to 90 percent uranium oxide by weight. Yellowcake can be refined even further until it is pure enough to be used as a nuclear fuel.

## TEXT-DEPENDENT QUESTIONS

1.  How do engineers use in situ leach mining to extract uranium?
2.  How do engineers use heap leaching to extract uranium?
3.  How can mineralogists detect uranium deposits?

## RESEARCH PROJECT

Use the library or the Internet to find out more about how uranium is mined, milled, refined, and then used. Create a flow chart showing the various stages.

## Chapter Three

# SCIENCE AND USES

I f you had a super-powerful microscope that could gaze inside an atom of uranium, you'd see an atom of 92 positively charged protons and an equal number of negatively charged electrons. That's significantly more than any other element. These subatomic particles are what give uranium its atomic heft.

### Words to Understand

**ballistic:** relating to the movement of objects propelled through the air.

**degrade:** break down.

**fossil fuels:** sources of fuel, such as oil and coal, that contain carbon and come from the decomposed remains of prehistoric plants and animals.

Like other elements, uranium comes in various forms, known as isotopes, each differing in the number of uncharged particles, or neutrons. Uranium atoms have between 143 to 146 neutrons. But, unlike other atoms, uranium atoms contain a tremendous source of power.

## Nuclear Reactions

This power comes in the form of nuclear reactions. If you were to use your microscope to look deeper, you'd also see that the uranium atom is very unstable.

The three cooling towers of a nuclear power plant.

In fact, it is so unstable that even the nuclear force that binds all the protons and neutrons has a tough time doing its job. If you were to look extremely close, you'd see protons and neutrons escaping from the atom at tremendous speeds, which makes uranium unstable. As they escape, they create an invisible electromagnetic force we call radioactivity.

> ## Uranium by the Numbers
>
> Atomic number: 92
> Atomic symbol: U
> Atomic weight: 238.03
> Phase at room temperature: solid
> Melting point: 2,075°F (1,135°C)
> Boiling point: 7,468°F (4,131°C)

You cannot talk about uranium without talking about radioactivity. Nuclear bombs can unleash a tremendous amount of nuclear radiation. An atomic bomb explosion is an uncontrolled nuclear reaction.

Yet radioactivity also comes in the form of a spontaneous nuclear reaction, meaning it takes place without the help of an outside trigger. During a spontaneous nuclear reaction, unstable elements, such as uranium, continue to emit radiation until they achieve a relatively harmless stable state. In other words, uranium loses bits and pieces of itself over time. As it does so, it **degrades** into other elements, such as thorium, until it becomes lead.

The instability of uranium atoms also makes the element a very special source of energy. Because uranium atoms have so many neutrons, they can easily split into two lighter atoms when struck by other neutrons. The chances of this happening are good. A pound of uranium has trillions of atoms with trillions of neutrons, which will eventually smash into other uranium atoms. When that happens, an enormous

## The First Nuclear Power Plants

On December 20, 1951, a uranium-powered nuclear reactor in Idaho began generating electricity in the town of Arco. The reactor was not very big, but it was the first time a nuclear reaction powered a light bulb—or four light bulbs, to be exact.

Three years later, in the Russian town of Obninsk, a nuclear power plant called APS 1 went online. It generated five megawatts of electricity as the world's first commercial nuclear power plant. By 2013 there were 437 nuclear power plants in 31 countries, according to the European Nuclear Society.

amount of energy shoots out from the atom in the form of heat. The process is called nuclear fission.

When a uranium atom undergoes fission, it releases neutron after neutron. Those neutrons slam into atom after atom, much like marbles banging into one another. Those atoms split in a chain reaction.

## Nuclear Power

Controlling this chain reaction is quite a feat. A controlled nuclear reaction can create electricity that can light up entire towns. The first controlled nuclear reaction occurred on December 2, 1942, in Chicago. A team of scientists, led by the Italian physicist Enrico Fermi, demonstrated the reaction in a reactor they built on a squash court at the University of Chicago.

**Physicist Enrico Fermi.**

The first reactor did not look like any of today's nuclear reactors. It was constructed of graphite blocks packed with uranium oxide and uranium metal stacked 57 layers high. No one knew what would happen when the nuclear reaction was put in motion. A three-person "suicide squad" waited to rush into the reactor and shut it down in case things went horribly wrong.

## A Revolutionary Equation

$E=mc^2$ is the most famous math equation in history. It is important because it gives scientists the ability to understand many things, including how to develop nuclear energy. But do you know what it really means? E stands for energy, m stands for mass, and c stands for the speed of light.

Einstein, who came up with the equation, said the energy contained in any object is equal to its mass multiplied by the speed of light squared—a huge number. Einstein said all objects contain energy. For example, the energy packed into the mass of one raisin could supply enough power for most of New York City for one day. If mass contains energy, then energy must have mass, which is why, Einstein said, the Sun's rays have mass, just like any other object.

Fortunately for the more than 50 people in attendance that day, the reactor worked as planned. The scientists watched in amazement as the Nuclear Age was born. That first experiment led to the creation of the atomic bomb, and later to nuclear power plants.

Nuclear power plants use controlled nuclear reactions to generate electricity by boiling water. Inside a nuclear power plant, the energy emitted by the splitting of uranium atoms heats the water. The steam from the superheated water then turns huge fanlike machines called turbines that drive generators. Those generators produce electricity.

Nuclear reactors are very efficient at generating electricity. The energy from one atom of uranium produces 10 million times the energy than an atom of carbon found in coal, a **fossil fuel**. In fact, one ton of uranium produces more energy than several million tons of coal or millions of barrels of oil. As such, nuclear power plants need less fuel than fossil-fuel power plants.

Today, nuclear power accounts for about 19 percent of all the electricity generated in the United States. Inside a nuclear power plant, nuclear reactions have to be carefully controlled. If workers allow fission to subside, the nuclear reaction will die down. If workers allow too much fission to take place, the nuclear reaction might get out of control.

## Nuclear Medicine

Uranium also has the ability to heal. Some uranium isotopes are used in diagnosing and treating certain medical conditions, including various forms of cancer.

During so-called radiation therapy, doctors treat patients using high-energy particles, including X-rays, gamma rays, protons, or other types of radiation, to destroy or damage cancer cells that can grow uncontrollably.

Some forms of radiation treatment can be applied externally. In other words, a special machine directs the radiation onto a cancerous tumor and the surrounding tissue. External radiation treatment can take several forms, including the following:

- **Three-dimensional conformal radiation therapy (3D-CRT)**. This therapy bombards the cancer with radiation from different directions in a precise

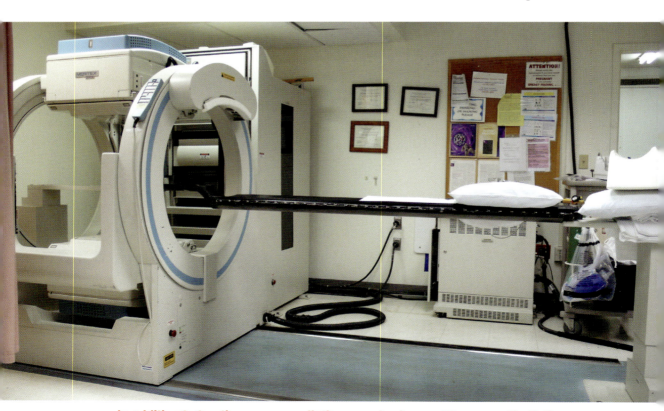

In addition to treating cancer, radiation can also be used to scan patients for any cancer that may be developing in bones or organs.

way. This allows doctors and technicians to aim the beams of radiation more accurately, which can reduce the damage to healthy tissue and cells.

- **Intensity-modulated radiation therapy (IMRT)**. IMRT works somewhat like three-dimensional therapy, yet it can change the strength of the beams to give some areas larger doses of radiation.

- **Conformal proton beam radiation therapy**. This form of radiation therapy slams beams of protons into cancerous cells. The protons do little damage to the tissue they pass through, but are very good at killing cancer cells. Protons can only be produced by special machines call cyclotrons and synchrotrons.

Sometimes, doctors also treat cancer patients with internal radiation therapy, in which the radiation source is put inside a patient's body.

## Nuclear Weapons

Ever since the first nuclear bomb exploded over Hiroshima on August 6, 1945, many countries have sought to develop nuclear weapons of their own. At the time of the Hiroshima blast, the United States was the world's only nuclear power. Today, nine countries can deliver a nuclear warhead on **ballistic** missiles. Although the politics of atomic weapons have changed over the decades, the science of building an atomic bomb has not.

While some nuclear weapons, such as hydrogen bombs, rely on fusion, fission is still at the heart of many weapons. For scientists to use uranium in a nuclear weapon, they need to enrich the element to a "weapons-grade" material. That means that the uranium fuel has to be composed of at least 90 percent U-235, which is a highly fissionable material. By contrast, when uranium is taken from the ground, it only consists of about 0.7 percent U-235. What does that mean? Enriching uranium to such levels increases the proportion of atoms. Remember what Einstein said: the more atoms you have, the more mass you have. The more matter you have, the more energy you can create. That's why U-235 is one of the best materials to go inside an atomic weapon. Moreover, it is easy for an atom of U-235 to grab hold of a neutron and eject other neutrons during fission.

The first missile to carry a live nuclear warhead was the PGM-11 Redstone. This ballistic missile is now a monument in the center of Warren, New Hampshire.

The *U.S.S. Nautilus* in New York City, 1958.

Uranium can also be used a source of fuel for warships, including aircraft carriers and submarines. As with the atomic bomb, the United States developed the world's first nuclear-powered submarine. On January 21, 1954, the US Navy's USS *Nautilus* set sail. Onboard the ship, which was named in honor of Captain Nemo's submarine in Jules Verne classic novel *Twenty Thousand Leagues under the Sea*, was a nuclear reactor that provided the ship with electricity.

Up until that point, most submarines had to surface to recharge their electric batteries. The *Nautilus*, however, could remain underwater indefinitely. The nuclear reactor worked just like a nuclear power plant, using super-heated water to generate electricity.

## Out of This World

Since the 1960s, NASA, the space agency of the United States, has been launching nuclear-powered ships into outer space. Military satellites were the first. These days, NASA scientists are trying to figure out how to build a nuclear-fission engine that could propel a spaceship to Mars and beyond. NASA has been using plutonium, a radioactive element created when uranium atoms absorb neutrons, as a source of fuel for years.

## TEXT-DEPENDENT QUESTIONS

1. What are some forms of electromagnetic radiation?
2. Why do scientists use uranium as a source of power?
3. How does $E=mc^2$ relate to nuclear energy?

## RESEARCH PROJECT

Nuclear power is a form of alternative energy that can be used to power homes and factories. Research and create a photographic essay on other forms of alternative energy sources, comparing them to fossil fuels. Publish your essay as a booklet or as computer slide show.

## Chapter Four

# COMMERCE AND ECONOMICS

**U**ranium is big business in many areas, but the economics can sometimes conflict with the environmental impact of mining the element. The people of Pittsylvania County, Virginia, know this better than anyone. During the height of the **recession** in 2009, Pittsylvania County was suffering. The county's unemployment rate skyrocketed to 12.1 percent. That number dropped to just under 7 percent in the summer of 2014, but the county still had one of the highest jobless rates in the state.

### Words to Understand

**indigenous:** growing or living naturally in a particular region or environment.

**recession:** a temporary economic downturn during which trade and industrial activity are reduced.

**reserves:** amounts in store, which can be used in the future.

**speculators:** risk-taking investors with expertise in the markets in which they trade.

Life was hard for many people in the county. Some looked to the summit of Coles Hill for a solution. Atop the hill in the town of Chatham sat an old plantation house that looked down on lush fields that once grew tobacco. Under the hill and under those green pastures, however, sat one of the largest uranium oxide deposits in North America. If the uranium was removed and refined, it could yield a significant amount of yellowcake—roughly 119 million pounds (54 million kilos). The mining company, Virginia Uranium, Inc., had wanted to mine the area for decades. Many people said mining Coles Hill would create an economic boon for Pittsylvania County. Experts said the mine would support 1,000 jobs annually over a 35-year period, providing $135 million each year to the state and local economy.

The mine, which could be worth up to $10 billion, would therefore be an economic windfall to an otherwise depressed area. But many people protested the plan, fearing a uranium mine would make their property worthless and cause many health problems. For many of those living near Coles Hill, the economics of uranium mining weren't worth the risks. Many peopled joined forces with environmentalists to keep a 1982 ban on mining in the area in place. "This is going to affect everybody that lives in these communities," one local resident once told a reporter. "This is something you leave alone."

## The Economics of Uranium Mining

Whether it's gold, copper, uranium, or silver, mining is one of the most important industries in society. Without it, the tools and products we use every day, everything from our cell phones to our cars, would not exist. Yet uranium mining is a difficult business, not just for the companies who invest millions in the hopes of turning a profit, but for many others, too.

For one thing, uranium is in short supply. The quest to find more of the element has brought mining companies to remote areas. These large mining operations often affect **indigenous** societies, harming the environment and destroying ways of life. In one corner of India, for example, the government has faced much opposition in its attempt to open a uranium mine close to the border of Bangladesh. To win the residents over, the government has promised to build schools and hospitals, and to create

## Uranium Demand in the United States

Nuclear power plants generate 20 percent of the electricity in the United States. But only 9 percent of the uranium used is produced domestically. Most of the uranium for those reactors is imported from other countries, including Canada (20 percent), Russia (19 percent), Kazakhstan (18 percent), Namibia (11 percent), and Australia (11 percent).

much-needed jobs. But for many of those living in the region, saying yes to uranium means saying yes to development and a substantial change in their way of life.

When all the uranium has been removed and the mines shut down, communities that once relied on the mines for jobs and economic opportunity are often left with environmental problems and a high jobless rate. The United States was once the world's top uranium producer. It now imports more than 90 percent of the yellowcake that the nation's 104 nuclear power reactors use as a source of fuel.

A uranium mine in northern Australia. There has been controversy over the siting of uranium mines on indigenous peoples' land.

## Top Six Uranium-Producing Nations

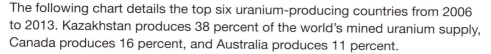

The following chart details the top six uranium-producing countries from 2006 to 2013. Kazakhstan produces 38 percent of the world's mined uranium supply, Canada produces 16 percent, and Australia produces 11 percent.

### Production from Mines (in metric tons)

| Country | 2006 | 2007 | 2008 | 2009 | 2010 | 2011 | 2012 | 2013 |
|---|---|---|---|---|---|---|---|---|
| Kazakhstan | 5,279 | 6,637 | 8,521 | 14,020 | 17,803 | 19,451 | 21,317 | 22,574 |
| Canada | 9,862 | 9,476 | 9,000 | 10,173 | 9,783 | 9,145 | 8,999 | 9,332 |
| Australia | 7,593 | 8,611 | 8,430 | 7,982 | 5,900 | 5,983 | 6,991 | 6,350 |
| Niger (est) | 3,434 | 3,153 | 3,032 | 3,243 | 4,198 | 4,351 | 4,667 | 4,528 |
| Namibia | 3,067 | 2,879 | 4,366 | 4,626 | 4,496 | 3,258 | 4,495 | 4,315 |
| Russia | 3,262 | 3,413 | 3,521 | 3,564 | 3,562 | 2,993 | 2,872 | 3,135 |

*Source:* World Nuclear Association, http://www.world-nuclear.org/info/Nuclear-Fuel-Cycle/Mining-of-Uranium/World-Uranium-Mining-Production/.

Still, for other communities, uranium mining has been an economic savior. While the United States had only nine working uranium mines in 2010, Canada is rich in uranium. In 2008, Canada was the world's largest producer of uranium. (Kazakhstan earned the top spot the following year.)

In Canada, Saskatchewan is the largest producer of uranium, and many people there owe their livelihoods to the element. In 2012 the uranium mining industry spent an estimated $377 million on salaries and benefits for its employees in Saskatchewan, while contractors hired by the mining companies paid out an additional $255 million. Moreover, Saskatchewan's uranium mining companies paid $166.9 million to the province and $5.7 million to local governments. Although other countries produce the most uranium, Australia has the world's largest uranium **reserves**, estimated in 2011 to be 1.66 million tons. Kazakhstan has 50 known uranium deposits, while Russia in 2013 was the world's sixth biggest uranium producing country.

## A Unique Element

Uranium is not like other minerals, such as gold, silver, and copper, all of which have a variety of uses. For all practical purposes, uranium can only be used in two industries—military technology and the generation of nuclear power.

Between 1942, when the first controlled nuclear reaction took place, and 1974, at the height of the Cold War, the world's militaries used 200,000 tons of uranium—roughly 50 percent of the total world output during that period. The world has changed a lot since then. The military uses of uranium have taken a back seat to nuclear power production.

Uranium is unique among the elements because there is no direct substitute. No fuel can replace uranium in a nuclear power plant. Across the globe, about 435 nuclear power reactors use about 78,000 tons of yellowcake, containing about 66,000 tons of mined uranium. Like any other commodity, the need for uranium fluctuates with demand. The demand for nuclear power has slowed in recent years because reactors now run more efficiently, depressing the demand for uranium.

Yet uranium mine production has historically not kept up with the demand of the nuclear power industry. The annual global consumption of uranium is 190 million pounds, while annual global mine production is 140 million pounds. To help close that gap, the United States and Russia began a "Megaton to Megawatts" program in 1993. This program has been able to fill that shortfall by supplying 9,000 tons of uranium each year. The program converts the highly enriched uranium from old Soviet atomic weapons to uranium that nuclear power plants can use.

## Ups and Downs

Since the early 2000s, the price for uranium has fluctuated wildly. In 2003, the price of a pound of uranium was $10. In mid-2007 the price skyrocketed to $135, but then it crashed to $40. The rise was driven by **speculators**, who invested heavily in uranium. The collapse was fueled by the global economic crisis, which began late in 2007 and lasted until 2009.

## Waste Disposal

One big concern with nuclear power is how to dispose of radioactive leftovers. One method is referred to as KBS-3; it is a fairly new technology that is planned for use in disposal sites currently under construction in Sweden and Finland. KBS-3 involves putting the spent fuel in a boron steel canister (on the right side of the photo), which then goes inside a copper casing (on the left). The sealed canister is then buried, where it will remain for 100,000 years. Some controversy exists, however, about whether the copper casing will be able to hold out for that many years.

**The KBS-3 method of spent uranium storage.**

Then in 2011, disaster struck. A 9.0 magnitude earthquake and 42.65 foot (13 meter) tsunami rocked northeastern Japan, creating a nuclear disaster at the country's Fukushima power plants. At the time, Japan operated 55 nuclear power plants, or 12 percent of the total number of power plants in the world. Prior to the disaster, the price of uranium was more than $72 per pound. After the quake, the price plummeted because the Japanese government forced the shutdown of all of Japan's nuclear reactors. By the summer of 2014, the price of uranium was just over $31 a pound.

That price could rise once again over the next decade, as more than 100 new nuclear reactors come on line, half in China. As a result, the Chinese will need about 44 million pounds of uranium each year by 2020. Much of it will be imported from other countries, because China's uranium mines will not be able to handle this increase.

## TEXT-DEPENDENT QUESTIONS

1. How much uranium does the United States import?
2. Why is there a shortage of uranium in the world?
3. Which country is the second-largest producer of mined uranium?

## RESEARCH PROJECT

Research whether there is a nuclear power plant in your community or state. Find out how much electricity it generates. Research which type of power reactor it has. Does it use boiling water, or does it use pressurized water? How many people live in a 50-mile (80-kilometer) radius of the plant? How many people work there? Have there been any accidents at the plant? If so, how many, and when? Create a chart showing all this information.

## Chapter Five

# URANIUM AND THE ENVIRONMENT

U ranium mining has been going on in Arizona since the early 20th century, but it really took off at the start of the Cold War in the 1950s. Over the ensuing decades, miners, especially those from the Navajo Nation, extracted some 4 million tons of uranium-rich ore, much of it used to make nuclear weapons for the US military.

### Words to Understand

**critical mass:** the minimum amount of fissile material needed to maintain a nuclear chain reaction.

**deplete:** to use up an available supply.

**half-life:** the amount of time it takes a radioactive substance to lose half of its atoms.

**ingest:** to swallow or absorb into the body.

While the miners made a good living, it came at a high cost. Over those years, many Navajo miners died from radiation-related illnesses. In part, this was because they used contaminated rock from the mine to build homes for their families. In 2007, US environmental officials began to assess the damage on Navajo land. Homeowners received government help in tearing down contaminated houses and building new ones in their place.

## Pollution and Rays

The story of the Navajo miners illustrates the environmental and health hazards associated with uranium mining. In many respects, uranium mining is just like the mining of any other element. As with these other elements, the impact on the

The Orphan Lode mine, just two miles west of the Grand Canyon, began life as a copper mine in 1893. It was abandoned a few years later, but reopened as a gold and uranium mine in 1956. The mine was closed again in 1969 after 13 million pounds (almost 6 million kilos) of uranium was extracted.

## Uranium Tailings

Uranium tailings contain more than a dozen radioactive materials, including thorium-230, radium-226, and radon-222. If the tailings are left to dry in the sun, the wind can blow the debris far from the mine, or rain can wash the tailings into lakes and rivers, further contaminating the environment.

**A photo from 1972 of the San Miguel River, contaminated by acid and radium 226, which leaked from a uranium tailings pond.**

environment can be great. However, uranium mines are unique because people can be exposed to radiation, which can cause health problems when the high-energy rays travel through a person's skin. But most of the problems occur when people accidentally **ingest** or inhale bits of uranium or other radioactive materials as they work. Studies have linked such elements as radium, which is found in uranium ore, to an increased risk of cancer.

Meanwhile, uranium mines can pollute groundwater and the air, affecting local plant and animal life. Uranium mining can also contaminate rivers and streams with radioactive particles and heavy metals. For these reasons, uranium mines have to go through a strict environmental assessment process to make sure mining companies are minimizing the risks.

Much of the environmental impact comes from tailing deposits—the materials that are left over after uranium is removed from its ore. Milling uranium ore so it can be made into fuel for nuclear reactors requires the use of many toxic chemicals. During that process, the waste rock, or tailings, which contain heavy metals such as radium, pile up in huge mounds.

It takes thousands of years for radium to decay, a process which scientists call **half-life**. As it does, the element produces a radioactive gas called radon, which can cause lung cancer. Radon was first discovered in 1900, and scientists began to classify it as a health risk in the late 1980s. Uranium mines are not the only source of the gas. Radon naturally seeps up from the ground and can accumulate in enclosed spaces.

Engineers often place tailings piles in large trenches or abandoned mine pits, where the radioactive elements and gases can be contained. Radon is not just a problem above the ground, but below the ground, too. Uranium mines must use complex ventilation systems to vent the gas, and miners must use protective gear when working in areas where there is a high concentration.

## Nuclear Accidents

Unlike fossil fuels, such as coal and oil, nuclear energy burns "clean" and does not pollute the atmosphere with harmful gases, such as carbon dioxide. However, sometimes things can go horribly wrong at a nuclear power plant, which can devastate the environment.

Nuclear reactors are designed for maximum safety, and it is very unlikely that one could explode like a nuclear bomb. Many dangers exist, however. For one thing, if workers allow too much fission to take place inside a reactor, the nuclear reaction might run out of control, causing the uranium fuel rods inside the protective core of the reactor to heat up. If the rods become too hot, the reactor can fail, releasing high doses of radioactive material into the environment. Such was the case in 1986, when an accident occurred at the Chernobyl nuclear reactor in the former Soviet Union. It was the world's worst nuclear mishap.

On April 26, 1986, the Chernobyl reactor exploded, sending a huge cloud of radioactivity into the atmosphere. The cloud drifted over much of Europe and badly contaminated a large part of Ukraine, Belarus, and Russia. Hundreds of thousands of people had to leave their homes.

A similar event very nearly occurred on March 28, 1979, at the Three Mile Island nuclear power plant near Middletown, Pennsylvania. In what so far has been worst nuclear disaster in the United States, a cooling malfunction caused part of the reactor's core to melt. Although some radioactive gas was released, it was not significant, and

**The ruins of a kindergarten in Pripyat, a city in Ukraine that had to be abandoned after the Chernobyl accident.**

**Aerial view of the Three Mile Island power plant in Pennsylvania. Unit 2 (left) was the source of the disaster in 1979 and has been permanently taken off line. Unit 1 (right) is still in use.**

there was no loss of life. Yet Three Mile Island was as a stark reminder of just how dangerous nuclear power reactors can be. The particular reactor that had the problem, called Unit 2, was permanently shut down, but the Three Mile Island plant itself is still operating.

Compared to Japan, the United States and Canada do not use a lot of nuclear energy. Thirty percent of Japan's electricity comes from nuclear power plants. On September 30, 1999, workers mixing liquid uranium at the Tokaimura nuclear plant accidentally triggered a chain reaction as they made fuel for the plant's nuclear reactor. Employees of the plant were working with U-235, which is a solid at room temperature. But if the temperature rises about 260°F (126°C), it turns into a dangerous gas. To keep the element from turning into a gas, the workers had to make U-235 into pellets by mixing the element with nitric acid.

On that day, workers mishandled the mixing process, dumping too much uranium into the acid. The mixture reached **critical mass**, which is the smallest amount of uranium needed to cause a chain reaction. Radiation levels spiked to 20,000 times the normal level. Luckily, the workers stopped the chain reaction before it caused too much damage.

Sometimes, though, humans aren't responsible for nuclear accidents. A 9.0 magnitude earthquake and tsunami struck Japan near the coastal city of Sendai on March 11, 2011. Eleven reactors at four different nuclear power plants shut down automatically when the quake hit, but the tsunami caused explosions at several reactors at the Fukushima Daiichi plant, located 40 miles (65 kilometers) south of Sendai. The result was a partial meltdown of several reactor units.

## Significant Nuclear Accidents

This chart includes information on the five worst nuclear accidents in history, based on information from the International Atomic Energy Agency (IAEA).

| Year | Location | Impact |
|---|---|---|
| 1952 | Chalk River, Canada | Mechanical and human errors led to an uncontrolled nuclear reaction, which led to a meltdown. The reactor and reactor building were heavily damaged after several hydrogen explosions. |
| 1957 | Kyshtym, Russia | There was a significant release of radiation after a nuclear waste tank exploded. |
| 1957 | Windscale Piles, United Kingdom | Radiation was released after a fire in a reactor core, contaminating milk from about 800 British farms. |
| 1986 | Chernobyl, Ukraine (Soviet Union) | There was a significant release of radiation from inside the reactor core, which caused widespread environmental damage. |
| 2011 | Fukushima, Japan | The reactors shutdown after a massive earthquake and tsunami, causing several explosions. |

It's important to remember that nuclear accidents are comparatively rare. According to the *Guardian* newspaper, there have only been 33 "serious" nuclear accidents. Of those, only two, Chernobyl and Fukushima, exposed the public to radiation doses that were greater than those resulting from exposure to natural radiation sources. When accidents do happen, they can be spectacular and severe, which is why many people are reluctant to invest in nuclear power despite its many benefits.

## Spent Fuel

One of the major problems with uranium is figuring out what to do with the element after it's been depleted. **Depleted** uranium is what's left over when most of the highly

Germans protest their government's nuclear power policies in 2010.

## Melting Down

The worst thing that can happen at a nuclear power plant is a *meltdown*. This term describes the overheating of the nuclear fuel, which can damage the core of a reactor. A meltdown occurs when the heat generated by the reactor is greater than the reactor's ability to cool it down. When the Fukushima Daiichi plant overheated, the reactors melted down, and the radiation split the water molecules into oxygen and hydrogen, resulting in a series of hydrogen explosions, which allowed radiation to escape.

**Inside the containment building of a nuclear reactor. Containment buildings are designed to keep radiation from leaking out of the reactor in the case of a meltdown.**

radioactive isotopes of uranium are removed for use as nuclear fuel or in nuclear weapons. Depleted uranium is stored at the enrichment plants. Some is also sold for commercial use, such as in military weapons. Individuals can be exposed to depleted uranium by breathing it in or by ingesting contaminated food or water. The consequences of this can be deadly.

For many people, depleted uranium is a sort of nuclear time bomb, just waiting to explode. The spent fuel from reactors are housed on-site at the power plants. The metal fuel rods, which are crammed with pellets of radioactive uranium dioxide, are stored in pools of water at the reactor site. The water draws away the leftover heat generated by the spent fuel, while also serving as a shield to protect workers from radiation.

Not that long ago, spent fuel rods were dumped in the ocean. That practice has since stopped. However, many people in the United States want to gather up all the

## Protecting a National Treasure

The Grand Canyon National Park is an American treasure. Every week, more than four million people travel to the area to peer over the canyon's rim to watch speculator sunrises and sunsets. So it was no surprise when the US Department of Interior, which oversees mining operations in the United States, decided to protect one million acres around the park from new uranium mining. The area, officials said, was both too culturally important and too environmentally sensitive to allow uranium to be extracted.

spent fuel from around the nation and put it in one storage facility where it could not harm the environment. The government scrapped plans to create such a facility at Yucca Mountain in Nevada because of environmental concerns, however.

The issue has been around for decades. In 1982, the US Congress passed a law directing the Energy Department to build a place to store nuclear waste, and five years later it amended the legislation, directing energy officials to determine whether Yucca Mountain could be turned into a safe storage facility. In 2010, President Barack Obama stopped the review process and asked a commission to recommend a new nuclear-waste disposal policy.

Many nuclear sites around the nation have had problems with the storage of nuclear waste. At the Los Alamos National Laboratory in New Mexico, where the first atomic bomb was detonated, a waste container leaked radiation in 2014. The container had a cracked lid and heat damage.

# TEXT-DEPENDENT QUESTIONS

1. What is depleted uranium?
2. How can radioactive materials from uranium mining make their way into the environment? Give three examples.
3. What is a nuclear meltdown?

# RESEARCH PROJECTS

1. Pick one of the nuclear accidents described in the text and create a slide presentation using photos and text that describes the accident and its aftermath in detail.
2. Research the ways in which people are exposed to four or five forms of electromagnetic radiation, and then create a chart detailing what overexposure to such radiation can mean to a person's health.

"To waste, to destroy, our natural resources, to skin and exhaust the land instead of using it so as to increase its usefulness, will result in undermining in the days of our children the very prosperity which we ought by right to hand down to them amplified and developed."

— Theodore Roosevelt
President of the United States (1901 to 1909)
Seventh Annual Message
December 3, 1907

# Further Reading

## BOOKS

Curie, Eve. *Madame Curie: A Biography*. 1937. Reprint, New York: Da Capo, 2001.

Gray, Theodore. *The Elements: A Visual Exploration of Every Known Atom in the Universe*. New York: Black Dog & Leventhal, 2009.

Isaacson, Walter. *Einstein: His Life and Universe*. New York: Simon & Schuster, 2007.

Kiernan, Denise. *The Girls of Atomic City. The Untold Story of the Women Who Helped Win World War II*. New York: Touchstone, 2013.

Pasternak, Judy. *Yellow Dirt: A Poisoned Land and the Betrayal of the Navajos*. New York: Free Press, 2010.

## ONLINE

History.com. "Albert Einstein." http://www.history.com/topics/albert-einstein.

Scientific American. "100 Years Ago: Marie Curie Wins 2nd Nobel Prize." http://www.scientificamerican.com/article/curie-marie-sklodowska-greatest-woman-scientist.

Voices of the Manhattan Project. http://manhattanprojectvoices.org.

# Series Glossary

**alloy:** mixture of two or more metals.

**alluvial:** relating to soil that is deposited by running water.

**aquicludes:** layers of rocks through which groundwater cannot flow.

**aquifer:** an underground water source.

**archeologists:** scientists who study ancient cultures by examining their material remains, such as buildings, tools, and other artifacts.

**biodegradable:** the process by which bacteria and organisms naturally break down a substance.

**biodiversity:** the variety of life; all the living things in an area, or on Earth on the whole.

**by-product:** a substance or material that is not the main desired product of a process but happens to be made along the way.

**carbon:** a pure chemical substance or element, symbol C, found in great amounts in living and once-living things.

**catalyst:** a substance that speeds up a chemical change or reaction that would otherwise happen slowly, if at all.

**commodity:** an item that is bought and sold.

**compound:** two or more elements chemically bound together.

**constituent:** ingredient; one of the parts of a whole.

**contaminated:** polluted with harmful substances.

**convection:** circular motion of a liquid or gas resulting from temperature differences.

**corrosion:** the slow destruction of metal by various chemical processes.

**dredge:** a machine that can remove material from under water.

**emissions:** substances given off by burning or similar chemical changes.

**excavator:** a machine, usually with one or more toothed wheels or buckets that digs material out of the ground.

**flue gases:** gases produced by burning and other processes that come out of flues, stacks, chimneys, and similar outlets.

**forges:** makes or shapes metal by heating it in furnaces or beating or hammering it.

**fossil fuels:** sources of fuel, such as oil and coal, that contain carbon and come from the decomposed remains of prehistoric plants and animals.

**fracking:** shorthand for hydraulic fracturing, a method of extracting gas and oil from rocks.

**fusion:** energy generated by joining two or more atoms.

**geologists:** scientists who study Earth's structure or that of another planet.

**greenhouse gas:** a gas that helps to trap and hold heat—much like the panes of glass in a greenhouse.

**hydrocarbon:** a substance containing only the pure chemical substances, or elements, carbon and hydrogen.

**hydrologic cycle:** events in which water vapor condenses and falls to the surface as rain, snow, or sleet, and then evaporates and returns to the atmosphere.

**indigenous:** growing or living naturally in a particular region or environment.

**inorganic:** compound of minerals rather than living material.

**kerogens:** a variety of substances formed when once-living things decayed and broke down, on the way to becoming natural gas or oil.

**leachate:** liquid containing wastes.

**mineralogists:** scientists who study minerals and how to classify, locate, and distinguish them.

**nonrenewable resources:** natural resources that are not replenished over time; these exist in fixed, limited supplies.

**ore:** naturally occurring mineral from which metal can be extracted.

**ozone:** a form of oxygen containing three atoms of oxygen in a molecule.

**porous:** allowing a liquid to seep or soak through small holes and channels.

**primordial:** existing at the beginning of time.

**producer gas:** a gas created ("produced") by industrial rather than natural means.

**reclamation:** returning something to its former state.

**reducing agent:** a substance that decreases another substance in a chemical reaction.

**refine:** to make something purer, or separate it into its various parts.

**remote sensing:** detecting and gathering information from a distance, for example, when satellites in space measure air and ground temperature below.

**renewable:** a substance that can be made, or a process used, again and again.

**reserves:** amounts in store, which can be used in the future.

**runoff:** water not absorbed by the soil that flows into lakes, streams, rivers, and oceans.

**seismology:** the study of waves, as vibrations or "shaking," that pass through the Earth's rocks, soils, and other structures.

**sequestration:** storing or taking something to keep it for a time.

**shaft:** a vertical passage that gives miners access to mine.

**sluice:** artificial water channel that is controlled by a value or gate.

**slurry:** a mixture of water and a solid that can't be dissolved.

**smelting:** the act of separating metal from rock by melting it at high temperatures

**subsidence:** the sinking down of land resulting from natural shifts or human activities.

**sustainable:** able to carry on for a very long time, at least the foreseeable future.

**synthesis:** making or producing something by adding substances together.

**tailing:** the waste product left over after ore has been extracted from rock.

**tectonic:** relating to the structure and movement of the earth's crust.

**watercourse:** a channel along which water flows, such as a brook, creek, or river.

# Index

(page numbers in *italics* refer to photographs and illustrations)

## About the Author

**John Perritano** is an award-winning journalist, writer, and editor from Southbury, Connecticut. He has written numerous articles and books on history, culture, and science for publishers that include National Geographic's Reading Expedition Series and its Global Issues Series. He has also contributed to Discovery.com, *Popular Mechanics,* and other magazines and Web sites. He holds a master's degree in American history from Western Connecticut State University.

## Photo Credits

### Cover

Clockwise from left: Dollar Photo Club/anibal; Dollar Photo Club/wellphoto; iStock.com/Uko_Jesita; Dollar Photo Club/marcel; iStock.com/overcrew; iStock.com/shujaa777; Wikimedia Commons: Fice.

### Interior

**Dollar Photo Club:** 22 wellphoto; 23 Scott Prokop; 28 Aneese; 39 vencav; 40 169169.

**Federal Emergency Management Agency:** 24.

**iStock.com:** 20 abadonian; 34 ArtPhaneuf; 49 abezikus; 50 Dobresum.

**Library of Congress:** 10 Harris & Ewing; 14; 16; 35.

**NASA:** 19 Chandra X-Ray Observatory.

**Nuclear Regulatory Commission:** 53.

**US Department of Energy:** 30.

**Wikimedia Commons:** 12 Geomartin; 13 instrumentmakers; 25; 32 liz west; 43 kallerna; 46 Alan Levine; 47 Bill Gillette; 52 Fice.